Fibro & Me:
Faith in the Midst of Pain

MONTHLY EDITION

This planner belongs to:

Fibro & Me:
Faith in the Midst of Pain

MONTHLY PLANNER

January - December 2021

JANUARY

S	M	T	W	T	F	S
					1	2
3	4	5	6	7	8	9
10	11	12	13	14	15	16
17	18	19	20	21	22	23
24	25	26	27	28	29	30
31						

FEBRUARY

S	M	T	W	T	F	S
	1	2	3	4	5	6
7	8	9	10	11	12	13
14	15	16	17	18	19	20
21	22	23	24	25	26	27
28						

MARCH

S	M	T	W	T	F	S
	1	2	3	4	5	6
7	8	9	10	11	12	13
14	15	16	17	18	19	20
21	22	23	24	25	26	27
28	29	30	31			

APRIL

S	M	T	W	T	F	S
				1	2	3
4	5	6	7	8	9	10
11	12	13	14	15	16	17
18	19	20	21	22	23	24
25	26	27	28	29	30	

MAY

S	M	T	W	T	F	S
						1
2	3	4	5	6	7	8
9	10	11	12	13	14	15
16	17	18	19	20	21	22
23	24	25	26	27	28	29
30	31					

JUNE

S	M	T	W	T	F	S
		1	2	3	4	5
6	7	8	9	10	11	12
13	14	15	16	17	18	19
20	21	22	23	24	25	26
27	28	29	30			

JULY

S	M	T	W	T	F	S
				1	2	3
4	5	6	7	8	9	10
11	12	13	14	15	16	17
18	19	20	21	22	23	24
25	26	27	28	29	30	31

AUGUST

S	M	T	W	T	F	S
1	2	3	4	5	6	7
8	9	10	11	12	13	14
15	16	17	18	19	20	21
22	23	24	25	26	27	28
29	30	31				

SEPTEMBER

S	M	T	W	T	F	S
			1	2	3	4
5	6	7	8	9	10	11
12	13	14	15	16	17	18
19	20	21	22	23	24	25
26	27	28	29	30		

OCTOBER

S	M	T	W	T	F	S
					1	2
3	4	5	6	7	8	9
10	11	12	13	14	15	16
17	18	19	20	21	22	23
24	25	26	27	28	29	30
31						

NOVEMBER

S	M	T	W	T	F	S
	1	2	3	4	5	6
7	8	9	10	11	12	13
14	15	16	17	18	19	20
21	22	23	24	25	26	27
28	29	30				

DECEMBER

S	M	T	W	T	F	S
			1	2	3	4
5	6	7	8	9	10	11
12	13	14	15	16	17	18
19	20	21	22	23	24	25
26	27	28	29	30	31	

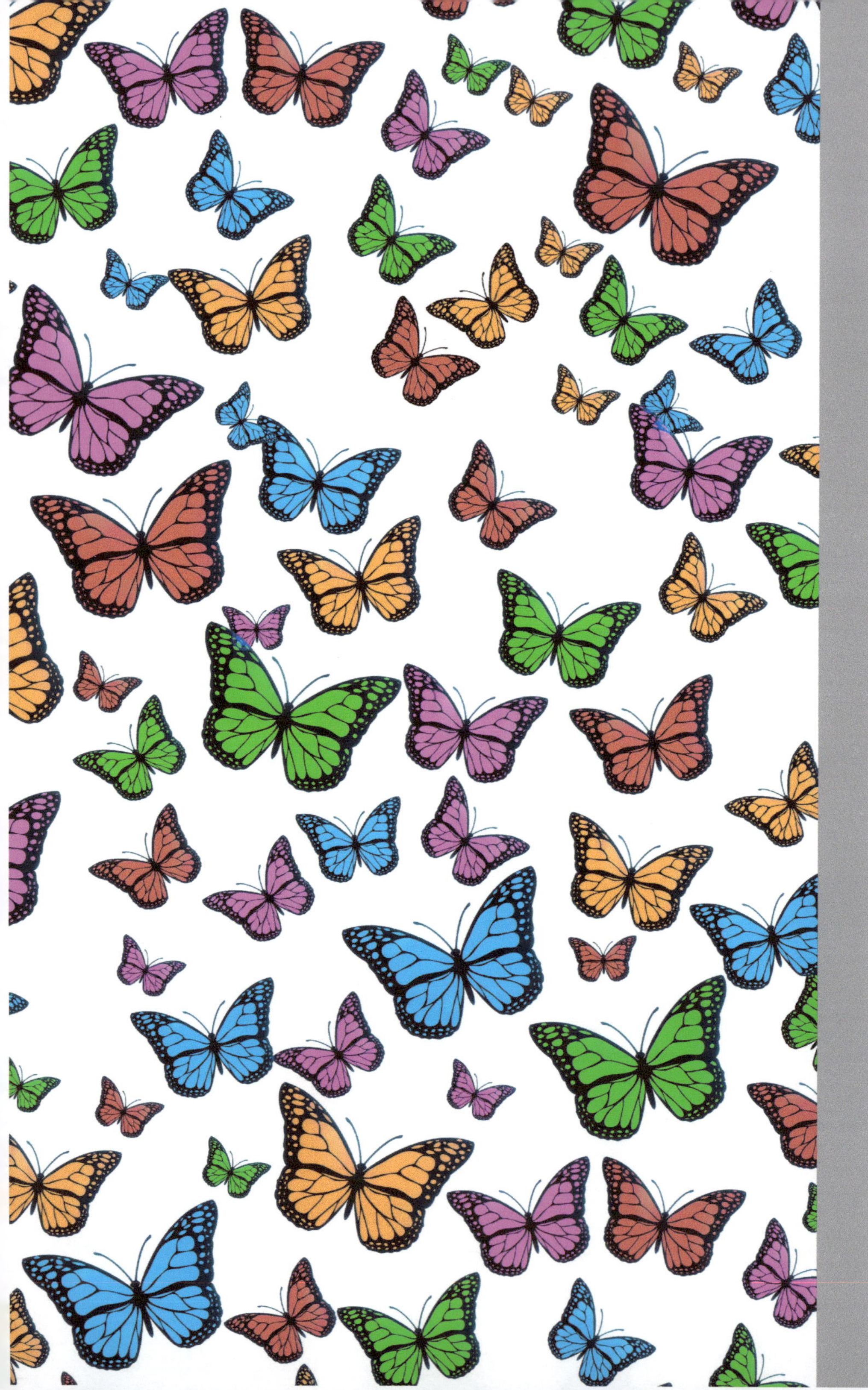

What's In Your Fibro & Me Planner

This planner is specifically designed to help y
manage your Fibromyalgia where you are a
continue to manage it where you're goi
I'm excited to take this journey with you.

- Hello Fibro Fighter!
- **Commit to Your Journey**
- A Letter to Myself
- Your Fibro Dream...
- Describe Your Best Fibro Day
- 2021 Goal Setting
- Quarterly Fibro Checklists:
  Four checklists designed to record questions to a
  your Fibro specialist, their recommendations, a
  update your medication list throughout the year.
- **Every month you will receive:**
  A monthly theme
  Foundational scripture
  Monthly Intentions (goals, to-do-list, etc.)
  Fibro Facts

Enjoy my fellow Fibro Fighter

Hello Fibro Fighter!

Welcome to the first day of the rest of your life wherever you are. You are about to embark on a beautiful new chapter of your life's journey. So are you going to close your eyes and hope for the best? Or are you going to get clear? This year I'm inviting you to set some intentions for the next twelve months. It's not about perfection, about getting things right or chasing an invisible ideal. Instead, it's about living with purpose every single day. Where's the best place to start? Exactly where you're at right now. So get yourself a cup of tea, clear some space around you, and then get started on the next page. Now, it might feel like you are alone at this, but please know that you are just one of many who are taking time out to Imagine their new year. Each with their own hopes and dreams for the future. So, let's get started, shall we?

With love,

Tabatha McC. Strother

Commit to Your Journey

THE CHOICE TO CHANGE

When you were a little child, you learned what it meant to be you from the people around you, the places you lived, and the experiences you had. All of those things brought you to who you are today. As you sit here, right now, you're about to embark on a whole new chapter in your life. Some things will stay the same. But most things will change. As you know, people will come and go. Experiences will be had and memories will be made. But you've been given a gift at this moment to decide. What you will do, how you will live with FM and who will you become through this journey? It's a new start, towards the next part of your journey of living with fibromyalgia and chronic pain. And sure. Things could stay the same. You could stop here, refuse to grow, and remain stuck. But at this moment, with this breath, you have a chance to say yes. Not to yourself, but to the you that you were meant to be. The one who is waiting for you to step out, stand up and commit to yourself, once and for all. So, are you ready for the next step?

A Letter To Myself

———————

Dear _____________,

It's time. I am ready to let go of the old, commit to myself and embrace change. I believe that the world around me is transformed by the renewing of my mind, the words I speak, and the choices I make. I know that my life is important. My words, thoughts, and actions are powerful.

So I am open to becoming more __________________ and choose to do more __________________. I am ready to commit to releasing my old stories about who I am and what I am capable of because _____________________.

This year I am going to be ________________. I'm going to spend more time with _____________, ______________, ______________ doing things like ______________, ______________, & _____________.

I am also going to devote myself to spending less time doing things that waste my precious time like _____________, _____________, & ____________ because they make me feel _____________, _____________, & ____________.

The top three things that are important to me are:

1.

2.

3.

...and I am ready to make them a priority in my life. No matter what.

One last thing: I love you and appreciate you ______________, because of all of the amazing things you have made it through and all the incredible things you have accomplished. Especially that time you __________________________.

I wish for you a life worth living, my friend. And I'll be here with you, until the end.

With love,

Your Fibro Dream...

You have what you say and you say what you see!

You know in movies when the main character rolls out of bed to the sound of their alarm clock? Annoying right? I feel the same way. But you know what? It doesn't have to be that way. In fact, it shouldn't be. Your life shouldn't be something that you have to be forced into. Even when times are tough, there should always be something to look forward to. That perfect cup of coffee, the call from a friend, the sound of the birds outside your window, or the feeling you get when you finally hit your goal. Most of us have been told that life is hard and it's supposed to be. That there isn't anything worth looking forward to. And to simply just get by. But I believe so much more is possible for us all and I know you do too. So I want you to take some time to write out your dream day. How would you feel? Who would you be spending it with? What would you do? Where would you live? How would you dress? Imagine what it could be like, not to have to take any meds or be concerned about Fibro or pain. This will help you start to make little changes to create that life for yourself. One day at a time.

Describe Your Best Fibro Day

A Fibromyalgia or Fibro Day is any day that you have to juggle your pain and your to do list. Take a deep breath, before you begin. I want you to close your eyes and think about what it is you would want that day to look and feel like. Yes, what do YOU want? Write down the details below. Be as vivid and descriptive as you possibly can!

____

____

____

____

____

____

____

____

____

____

____

2021 Yearly Goal Setting

FIBRO AND ME

This is the place to explore how you want to feel, what you want to do, and who you want to become in the next year of your life. Write down each of your goals in the following areas of your life.

EMOTIONAL GOALS	PHYSICAL GOALS	CREATIVE GOALS

FINANCIAL GOALS	SPIRITUAL GOALS	RELATIONAL GOALS

January
I AM
STRENGTHENED
FIBRO & ME | © 2021 TABATHA MCC. STROTHER

January Intentions

Date ___________________

I AM STRENGTHENED TO...

____

MONTHLY GOALS

-
-
-
-
-
-

DATES TO REMEMBER

TO DO LIST

- [ ] ______________________________
- [ ] ______________________________
- [ ] ______________________________
- [ ] ______________________________
- [ ] ______________________________
- [ ] ______________________________
- [ ] ______________________________
- [ ] ______________________________
- [ ] ______________________________
- [ ] ______________________________

Quarterly Fibro Check-In

Date ______________________

As you prepare for your quarterly appointment(s), be sure to write down the things you need to speak with your healthcare provider(s) about. After your appointment(s), write down any recommendations from your health care provider and update your medication list

QUESTIONS/CONCERNS FOR YOUR HEALTHCARE PROVIDER

MEDICATION LIST (CHECK THE BOX IF THE MEDICATION IS NEW OR THERE HAS BEEN A CHANGE)

HEALTHCARE PROVIDER RECOMMENDATIONS

January

ISAIAH 41:10

"Don't be afraid, for I am with you. Don't be discouraged for I am your God. I will strengthen you and help you. I will hold you up with my victorious right hand." (NLT)

SUN	MON	TUE	WED	THU	FRI	SAT
27	28	29	30	31	1 New Year's Day	2
3	4	5	6	7	8	9
10	11	12	13	14	15	16
17	18	19	20	21	22	23
24	25	26	27	28	29	30/31

Fibro Facts

Fibromyalgia affects approximately 4-5% of the U.S. population.
That's six to twelve million people of which 90% are women.

Today I feel...	*Things that help me to feel better...*	*My Prayers...*

February
I AM SAVED

February Intentions

Date ______________

I AM SAVED...

MONTHLY GOALS

DATES TO REMEMBER

TO DO LIST

- [ ] ______________________
- [ ] ______________________
- [ ] ______________________
- [ ] ______________________
- [ ] ______________________
- [ ] ______________________
- [ ] ______________________
- [ ] ______________________
- [ ] ______________________
- [ ] ______________________

February

JEREMIAH 17:14

"O Lord, if You heal me, I will be truly healed; if You save me, I will be truly saved. My praises are for you alone!" (NLT)

SUN	MON	TUE	WED	THU	FRI	SAT
31	1	2	3	4	5	6
7	8	9	10	11	12	13
14 Valentines Day	15	16	17	18	19	20
21	22	23	24	25	26	27
28						

Fibro Facts

Fibro fog or forgetfulness is one symptom associated with fibromyalgia that can be just as annoying as the pain itself. It's best to write things down.

Today I feel...

____

____

____

____

____

____

____

Things that help me to feel better...

____

____

____

____

____

____

____

My Prayers...

____

____

____

____

____

____

____

March
I AM RESTORED

March Intentions

Date ______________________

I AM RESTORED...

____

MONTHLY GOALS

DATES TO REMEMBER

TO DO LIST

☐ _______________________

☐ _______________________

☐ _______________________

☐ _______________________

☐ _______________________

☐ _______________________

☐ _______________________

☐ _______________________

☐ _______________________

☐ _______________________

March

PSALM 30:2

SUN	MON	TUE	WED	THU	FRI	SAT
28	1	2	3	4	5	6
7	8	9	10	11	12	13
14	15	16	17 St. Patrick's Day	18	19	20
21	22	23	24	25	26	27
28	29	30	31	1	2	3

Fibro Fact

Sleep disturbance is a major symptom of FM. This could be insomnia, waking during sleep, or not falling into a deep sleep. Sleep hygiene plays a major role in your FM care. Try playing soothing music, taking a relaxing bath, and unplugging from devices 45 minutes before bedtime to aid in getting a good night's sleep. Be sure to speak with your healthcare provider to discuss what works best for you.

Today I feel...	*Things that help me feel better...*	*My Prayers...*

April
I AM ALIVE

April Intentions

Date _______________

I AM ALIVE...

____

MONTHLY GOALS

-
-
-
-
-

DATES TO REMEMBER

TO DO LIST

- [ ] _______________________________
- [ ] _______________________________
- [ ] _______________________________
- [ ] _______________________________
- [ ] _______________________________
- [ ] _______________________________
- [ ] _______________________________
- [ ] _______________________________
- [ ] _______________________________
- [ ] _______________________________

Quarterly Fibro Check-In

Date _______________

As you prepare for your quarterly appointment(s), be sure to write down the things you need to speak with your healthcare provider(s) about. After your appointment(s), write down any recommendations from your health care provider and update your medication list

QUESTIONS/CONCERNS FOR YOUR HEALTHCARE PROVIDER

MEDICATION LIST (CHECK THE BOX IF THE MEDICATION IS NEW OR THERE HAS BEEN A CHANGE)

HEALTHCARE PROVIDER RECOMMENDATIONS

April

PROVERBS 4:20-22

"*My child, pay attention to what I say. Listen carefully to my words. Don't lose sight of them. Let them penetrate deep into your heart for they bring life to those who find them, and healing to their whole body.*" (NLT)

SUN	MON	TUE	WED	THU	FRI	SAT
28	29	30	31	1	2	3
4	5	6	7	8	9	10
11	12	13	14	15	16	17
18	19	20	21	22	23	24
25	26	27	28	29	30	

Fibro Facts

Be sure to take your medication(s) as prescribed by your healthcare provider. You and your healthcare provider should have discussed your condition and come up with a plan just for you; so be sure to follow it to get the maximum benefits.

Today I feel...

Things that make me feel better...

My Prayers...

May
I HAVE A
CHEERFUL HEART
FIBRO & ME | © 2021 TABATHA MCC. STROTHER

May Intentions

Date ________________

I HAVE A CHEERFUL HEART...

____

MONTHLY GOALS

- ⬡
- ⬡
- ⬡
- ⬡
- ⬡

DATES TO REMEMBER

TO DO LIST

- [ ] _______________________
- [ ] _______________________
- [ ] _______________________
- [ ] _______________________
- [ ] _______________________
- [ ] _______________________
- [ ] _______________________
- [ ] _______________________
- [ ] _______________________
- [ ] _______________________

May

PROVERBS 17:22

"A cheerful heart is good medicine, but a broken spirit saps a person's strength." (NLT)

SUN	MON	TUE	WED	THU	FRI	SAT
1/2	3	4	5	6	7	8
9	10	11	12	13	14	15
16	17	18	19	20	21	22
23	24	25	26	27	28	29
30	31					

Fibro Facts

Stress tends to intensify FM onsets and flare-ups. Be sure to minimize the amount of stress that you undertake whether mentally, emotionally, or physically. Finds ways to decompress.

Today I feel...	*Things that make me feel better...*	*My Prayers...*
________________	________________	________________
________________	________________	________________
________________	________________	________________
________________	________________	________________
________________	________________	________________
________________	________________	________________
________________	________________	________________
________________	________________	________________

June

ALL OF MY NEEDS
ARE SUPPLIED

June Intentions

Date ______________________

ALL OF MY NEEDS ARE SUPPLIED...

____

MONTHLY GOALS

⬡
⬡
⬡
⬡
⬡

DATES TO REMEMBER

TO DO LIST

☐ _______________________________
☐ _______________________________
☐ _______________________________
☐ _______________________________
☐ _______________________________
☐ _______________________________
☐ _______________________________
☐ _______________________________
☐ _______________________________
☐ _______________________________

June

PHILIPPIANS 4:19

SUN	MON	TUE	WED	THU	FRI	SAT
30	31	1 Independance Day	2	3	4	5
6	7	8	9	10	11	12
13	14	15	16	17	18	19
20	21	22	23	24	25	26
27	28	29	30	1	2	3

Fibro Facts

Exercise is a great way to loosen muscle tension and relieve pain.
Walking and/or stretching 3-5 days a week for at least 15 minutes
is a great technique and you may lose an inch or a pound along
the way.

Today I feel...

____

____

____

____

____

____

Things that make me feel better...

____

____

____

____

____

____

My Prayers...

____

____

____

____

____

____

July
I WALK IN
DISCIPLINE

July Intentions

Date ______________________

I WALK IN DISCIPLINE...

____

MONTHLY GOALS

DATES TO REMEMBER

TO DO LIST

☐ _______________________________

☐ _______________________________

☐ _______________________________

☐ _______________________________

☐ _______________________________

☐ _______________________________

☐ _______________________________

☐ _______________________________

☐ _______________________________

☐ _______________________________

Quarterly Fibro Check-In

Date ________________________

As you prepare for your quarterly appointment(s), be sure to write down the things you need to speak with your healthcare provider(s) about. After your appointment(s), write down any recommendations from your health care provider and update your medication list

QUESTIONS/CONCERNS FOR YOUR HEALTHCARE PROVIDER

MEDICATION LIST (CHECK THE BOX IF THE MEDICATION IS NEW OR THERE HAS BEEN A CHANGE)

HEALTHCARE PROVIDER RECOMMENDATIONS

July

ISAIAH 38:16

SUN	MON	TUE	WED	THU	FRI	SAT
27	28	29	30	1	2	3
4	5	6	7	8	9	10
11	12	13	14	15	16	17
18	19	20	21	22	23	24
25	26	27	28	29	30	31

Fibro Facts

A Tens Unit is a great non-invasive way to get relief from some muscle pain. However, you MUST consult with a healthcare provider to ensure that it's safe for you.

Today I feel...	*Things that make me feel better...*	*My Prayers...*
___________________	___________________	___________________
___________________	___________________	___________________
___________________	___________________	___________________
___________________	___________________	___________________
___________________	___________________	___________________
___________________	___________________	___________________
___________________	___________________	___________________

August

I AM HEALED FROM
ALL BROKENESS

August Intentions

Date ______________________

I AM HEALED FROM ALL BROKENESS...

____

MONTHLY GOALS

TO DO LIST

DATES TO REMEMBER

August

PSALM 147:3

SUN	MON	TUE	WED	THU	FRI	SAT
1	2	3	4	5	6	7
8	9	10	11	12	13	14
15	16	17	18	19	20	21
22	23	24	25	26	27	28
29	30	31	1	2	3	4

Fibro Facts

The foods we eat play a major role in flare-ups. Sugars, gluten, and dairy may have been a trigger for your latest flare-up. Try eating meals with less or no gluten, sugars, and dairy. Keep track of your flare-ups. You may find that you drop a few pounds in the process.

Today I feel...

____
____
____
____
____
____
____

Things that make me feel better...

____
____
____
____
____
____
____

My Prayers...

____
____
____
____
____
____
____

September

I AM REVIVED

September Intentions

Date ________________________

I AM REVIVED...

____

MONTHLY GOALS

-
-
-
-
-

DATES TO REMEMBER

TO DO LIST

- [ ] ______________________________
- [ ] ______________________________
- [ ] ______________________________
- [ ] ______________________________
- [ ] ______________________________
- [ ] ______________________________
- [ ] ______________________________
- [ ] ______________________________
- [ ] ______________________________
- [ ] ______________________________

September

PSALM 119:50

SUN	MON	TUE	WED	THU	FRI	SAT
29	30	31	1	2	3	4
5	6	7	8	9	10	11
Labour Day						
12	13	14	15	16	17	18
19	20	21	22	23	24	25
26	27	28	29	30	1	2

Fibro Facts

Some healthcare providers do not believe that FM is real. Be sure that your HCP takes you seriously, believes your complaints, and rules out other conditions such as Lupus, RA, and Lime Disease.

Today I feel...

____

____

____

____

____

____

____

Things that make ne feel better...

____

____

____

____

____

____

____

My Prayers...

____

____

____

____

____

____

October
I HAVE FAITH

October Intentions

Date ______________________

I HAVE FAITH...

____

MONTHLY GOALS

- ⬡
- ⬡
- ⬡
- ⬡
- ⬡

DATES TO REMEMBER

TO DO LIST

- ☐ ___________________________________
- ☐ ___________________________________
- ☐ ___________________________________
- ☐ ___________________________________
- ☐ ___________________________________
- ☐ ___________________________________
- ☐ ___________________________________
- ☐ ___________________________________
- ☐ ___________________________________
- ☐ ___________________________________

Quarterly Fibro Check-In

Date ________________________

As you prepare for your quarterly appointment(s), be sure to write down the things you need to speak with your healthcare provider(s) about. After your appointment(s), write down any recommendations from your healthcare provider and update your medication list

QUESTIONS/CONCERNS FOR YOUR HEALTHCARE PROVIDER

MEDICATION LIST (CHECK THE BOX IF THE MEDICATION IS NEW OR THERE HAS BEEN A CHANGE)

☐ ________________________

☐ ________________________

☐ ________________________

☐ ________________________

☐ ________________________

☐ ________________________

☐ ________________________

☐ ________________________

☐ ________________________

☐ ________________________

HEALTHCARE PROVIDER RECOMMENDATIONS

October

JAMES 5:15

SUN	MON	TUE	WED	THU	FRI	SAT
26	27	28	29	30	1	2
3	4	5	6	7	8	9
10	11 Columbus Day	12	13	14	15	16
17	18	19	20	21	22	23
24	25	26	27	28	29	30

Fibro Facts

It's vital for those suffering from FM or any chronic pain condition to keep a check on their mental health. Chronic pain can lead to lifestyle changes that in turn can lead to depression. Make therapy part of your pain management treatment.

Today I feel...

____

____

____

____

____

____

____

Things that make me feel better...

____

____

____

____

____

____

____

My Prayers...

____

____

____

____

____

____

____

November

I AM STRONG IN SPIRIT

November Intentions

Date _______________

I AM STRONG IN SPIRIT...

____

MONTHLY GOALS

DATES TO REMEMBER

TO DO LIST

- [ ] _______________________
- [ ] _______________________
- [ ] _______________________
- [ ] _______________________
- [ ] _______________________
- [ ] _______________________
- [ ] _______________________
- [ ] _______________________
- [ ] _______________________
- [ ] _______________________

November

3 JOHN 1:2

"*Dear friend, I hope all is well with you and that you are as healthy in body as you are strong in spirit.*" (NLT)

SUN	MON	TUE	WED	THU	FRI	SAT
31	1	2	3	4	5	6
7	8	9	10	11	12	13
14	15	16	17	18	19	20
21	22	23	24	25	26	27
28	29	30	1	2	3	4

Fibro Facts

Massage Therapy is another way to ease tension, relax your muscles, and relieve some pain due to FM. Seek a massage therapist who specializes in therapeutic massages.

Today I feel...	*Things that make me feel better...*	*My prayers...*

December

I AM HEALED

December Intentions

Date ________________

I AM HEALED...

____

MONTHLY GOALS

DATES TO REMEMBER

TO DO LIST

- ☐ ________________
- ☐ ________________
- ☐ ________________
- ☐ ________________
- ☐ ________________
- ☐ ________________
- ☐ ________________
- ☐ ________________
- ☐ ________________
- ☐ ________________
- ☐ ________________

December

ISAIAH 53:5

" But he was pierced for our rebellion, crushed for our sins. He was beaten so we could be whole. He was whipped so we could be healed." (NLT)

SUN	MON	TUE	WED	THU	FRI	SAT
28	29	30	1	2	3	4
5	6	7	8	9	10	11
12	13	14	15	16	17	18
19	20	21	22	23	24	25 Christmas Day
26	27	28	29	30	31	 New Years Day

Fibro Facts

Having a strong support system matters! Surrounding yourself with people who support you through this FM journey is just as important as your faith, doctors, and medications. Don't feel bad or ashamed if you have to cut some people off for your well being.

Today I feel...

____

____

____

____

____

____

____

Things that make me feel better...

____

____

____

____

____

____

____

My Prayers...

____

____

____

____

____

____

Yearly Review

This is the place to reflect on the goals you've been working on for the past year of your life. Write down your accomplishments in the spaces below to get clear on what you achieved and finally celebrate!

EMOTIONAL GOALS	PHYSICAL GOALS	CREATIVE GOALS

FINANCIAL GOALS	SPIRITUAL GOALS	RELATIONAL GOALS

For more information about Fibromyalgia, Chronic Pain.
and to find support groups in your area visit...

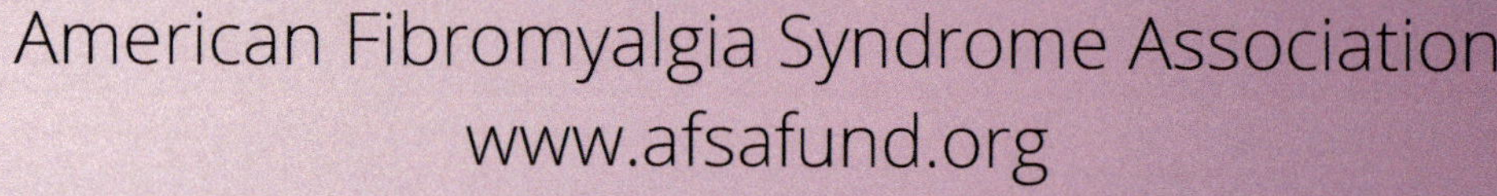

American Fibromyalgia Syndrome Association
www.afsafund.org

National Fibromyalgia Association
fmaware.net

National Fibromyalgia and Chronic Pain Association
www.fibroandpain.org

The American Chronic Pain Association
www.theacpa.org

Fibromyalgia Coalition International
www.fibrocaolition.org

About the Author

Tabatha Mcc. Strother is a licensed ordained minister. Tabatha is the founder of the African American Cultural Experience and the creator and host of the "Talking With Tabatha" podcast. She is also part of the Ministerial Staff at the Chester County Detention Center.

Tabatha has been an active member of the Fibromyalgia Community since 2003 after her Fibromyalgia diagnosis. Tabatha passionately advocates for research to lead to a better quality of living for those suffering from FM and prayerfully a cure. Her advocacy doesn't stop with FM. Tabatha advocates for her family #justiceforAraineMcCree, her community, and all those in need.

Follow me on Twitter
@EvanTab

Follow me on Instagram
@TalkingWithTabatha

Follow me on Facebook
@TalkingWithTabatha

"Pain may have gotten me here,
but the grace of God and faith will
get me through, so I am able to
journey onward."

TABATHA MCC. STROTHER

www.ingramcontent.com/pod-product-compliance
Lightning Source LLC
Chambersburg PA
CBHW042028050726

47599CB00005B/833